Nature Crafts

A Reader's Digest Young Families Book
Published by Joshua Morris Publishing, Inc.,
355 Riverside Avenue, Westport, CT 06880.
All rights reserved. Printed in Spain.

ISBN: 0-88705-976-7
1 3 5 7 9 10 8 6 4 2

Produced by Breslich & Foss

Volume copyright © 1996 by Breslich & Foss
Illustrations copyright © 1996 by Lyndsay Milne

Reader's Digest Young Families is a trademark of
The Reader's Digest Association, Inc.

Nature Crafts

Have fun with nature!
More than 80 great projects!

LYNDSAY MILNE

Reader's Digest Young Families

Westport, Connecticut

Contents

Introduction

Nature Crafts is packed with exciting projects to make and do. If you don't have your own garden, it doesn't matter—you can still sprout carrot tops, make a windmill, plant a bottle garden, build a caterpillar playground or tempt birds to your window. All you need are sharp eyes for spotting natural materials when you go for a walk in a park or in the country. At the beginning of each section, you will find a list of the other things you will need, and many of them—like empty cereal boxes or plastic containers—can be found around the house.

Many of the projects can be done indoors or outdoors, depending on the weather and how much space you have. If it's raining, there are plenty of indoor projects, ranging from making chocolate leaves to building a village hut. Most of the projects can be completed in a morning without any help from a grown-up. If you will need an adult's help, we'll tell you that in the instructions.

Throughout the book, you will find "Nature Facts" boxes. These are full of fascinating information about the world around us, from why it's windy at the seashore to how caterpillars breathe.

If you want to save pocket money, have fun and learn about the natural world, you'll find plenty of ideas in *Nature Crafts*.

Your nature collection

The sorts of things to collect are sticks, twigs, bark, acorns, seeds, beechnuts, pine cones, leaves, grasses, feathers and broken bits of pottery. At the beach, look out for empty shells, pebbles and nice pieces of driftwood that the sea has swept onto the sand. Keep all the things in your nature collection in jelly jars, plastic containers or shoe boxes so that you don't lose them.

Basic tool kit

These are things that you will need for many of the projects:

Pencil
Crayons
Black marker
Water-based paints
Paintbrushes
Masking tape
Craft glue
Scissors
Ruler
Double-sided tape

You will also need:

Plain paper, brown paper, colored paper, tissue paper, greaseproof paper, blotting paper, paper towels, and newspaper
Thick and thin cardboard, and corrugated cardboard
Large and small cardboard boxes and tubes
String or nylon thread
Wire hangers
Soft, malleable wire
Aluminum foil
Scraps of fabric
Stick pins
Dressmaker's elastic
Needle and thread
Plastic bottles, margarine tubs and yogurt containers
Jelly jars
Toothpicks
Sponge

Making things

In *Making things*, you will discover how to weave a nest from twigs and tell the time with your very own sundial.

What you will need:

Eggshells and egg cartons
Edible leaves and flowers
Dried beans, seeds and pasta
Dried and fresh herbs and spices
Fruit and vegetables
Cooking and baking pans
Ice cube tray
Corks
Cookie cutters   Thin wood
Candles   Bamboo stakes
Insulating tape   Grater
Beads   Muslin
Cotton balls   Baker's chocolate
Coconut   Balloons
Clear varnish   Photographic paper
Sheets of glass   Modeling clay
  or plastic   Plaster of Paris

How to make a flower press

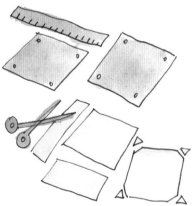

1 Ask an adult to cut two pieces of thin wood about 6 x 6 in (15 x 15 cm).

2 Ask the adult to tape the two squares together and drill a hole in each corner.

3 Untape the squares and cut a piece of cardboard and some pieces of blotting paper or greaseproof paper the same size. Cut off the corners so that they will fit within the holes.

How to press flowers and leaves

To make dried flowers and leaves for the projects, use a pile of heavy books or a flower press. Lay flowers and leaves between sheets of greaseproof paper or blotting paper and place them between the pages of a book. Close the book and stack some more heavy books on top of it. Leave the pile for two weeks or until the flowers and leaves have dried out.

4 Collect four wing nuts and four bolts. Push the bolts up through the holes. Lay down a piece of cardboard, then a sheet of blotting paper or greaseproof paper. Lay fresh leaves and flowers on top and cover with another sheet of paper.

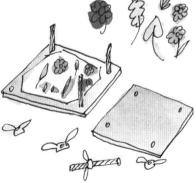

5 When you have finished building up all the layers of paper, leaves and flowers, place the other piece of wood on top. Screw down all of the wing nuts. Leave for two weeks.

Tips

Ask an adult which flowers and leaves you can pick. Some wildflowers are protected by law because they are rare. If you see just one example of a flower in the countryside, do not pick it! Only pick flowers when there are lots of them and be careful not to pull up the roots. Better still, buy wildflower seeds in packets and plant them in pots or outdoors.

Many people are allergic to pollen and wildflowers, so be very careful to wash your hands after handling. Stop handling the flowers if you begin to sneeze, your eyes become itchy, or your throat starts to feel scratchy.

When walking in the country or in a park, make sure that you don't leave litter behind. Litter is ugly and dangerous. Small animals can become trapped inside bottles and cut by broken glass. Both birds and animals can choke on scraps of plastic.

Make a list of all the ways that you use trees and plants throughout the day. What about the oats in your cereal, the cotton T-shirt you wear, the rubber on your bicycle tires, or the scent in your soap?

Flowers and leaves

You can do all kinds of things with flowers and leaves, from decorating a curtain to making chocolate shapes. Look out for flowers growing in strange places, such as between the cracks in brick walls.

Pressed flower card

1 Draw a person with one arm outstretched on a piece of thin cardboard. Color this in.

2 Carefully cut around the outline of the hand. Glue some pressed flowers with their stems behind the hand so that it looks like the figure is holding a bunch of flowers.

Leaf cards

With the blade tip of a closed pair of scissors, make a hole at the top of the cardboard. Thread a piece of string through the hole, and use the card as a gift tag.

1 Choose a pressed leaf and lay it on thin cardboard. Draw a rectangle or square bigger than the leaf and cut the shape out.

2 Draw a line down the middle of the rectangle and paint the right half. You can also cover one side with colored paper, glued to the paper and trimmed.

3 Paint the right half of the leaf white. When dry, glue it to the cardboard, making sure that the leaf's spine lines up with the center.

Skeleton leaves

3 Find a piece of cardboard that is twice as big as you want your card to be. Fold it in half. Paint the front a bright color. Glue the picture to the cardboard.

Keep an eye out for skeleton leaves. These are leaves that have rotted away, leaving just the veins that carry water and nutrients through the living leaf. Caterpillars are one of many types of insect that eat leaves. The veins are hard to chew, and so they are sometimes left. Leaf skeletons make beautiful gifts when glued onto white cardboard or hung between sheets of glass or hard, clear plastic.

Leaf silhouettes

This paper looks good taped to a sunny window or held in front of a lampshade where light can shine through it. But be careful not to hold the paper over a lampshade. The paper may burn!

1 Collect some leaves with interesting shapes. Lay one on a sheet of paper, holding it in place with your finger. Brush on paint from the middle to just over the edge of the leaf. That way you will not get paint under the leaf.

2 Remove the first leaf, then paint over another one with a different color.

3 Continue building a pattern with different shaped leaves.

Decorated box

1 Paint a chocolate box or a cigar box one color on the inside and another color on the outside. Let dry. Touch the box. If it's not sticky, it's dry.

2 Work out the design by arranging some pressed flowers and leaves in a pattern on the top of the box.

3 When you are happy with the pattern, apply a little glue to the back of each flower and leaf. Gently press them onto the box.

4 When the glue is dry, brush a clear coat of varnish over the box to make it shiny and to prevent the flowers and leaves from breaking. If the box is small, you can use clear nail polish.

Leaf plate

1 Collect some autumn leaves that are not too dried out. Use a small paper plate for small leaves and a large plate for big leaves. Grease the top of the plate by rubbing a little margarine or petroleum jelly over the surface.

2 Carefully paint some glue onto the back of one leaf with a brush. Lay it in the middle of the plate. Glue on more leaves so that their ends go beyond the edge of the plate. Keep the stems pointing to the center of the plate.

3 When the plate is completely covered, glue some scraps of newspaper on top of the leaves. Make sure they do not cover the leaves at the edge of the plate. Apply two or three layers of paper.

4 Now that you have strengthened the plate with paper, glue on enough leaves to cover the paper.

5 Finally, glue one or two more leaves to the middle of the plate to finish it off.

Nature Facts

Leaves contain a substance called chlorophyll, which turns sunlight into chemical energy. This process is called photosynthesis.

Photosynthesis converts carbon dioxide, which is the air we breathe out, into the oxygen we breathe in. It is chlorophyll that makes leaves green.

6 Find a china plate with a smooth bottom that will not leave a mark on the paper plate. Grease the bottom of the china plate. Clean off any excess glue from the leaves by gliding a damp sponge over them. Place the china plate onto the leaf-covered plate. Weigh them down with a pile of heavy books and leave for 12 hours. Gently peel the leaf-covered plate from the china plate.

Fox face leaf

1 Find a large, strong, three-pointed leaf.

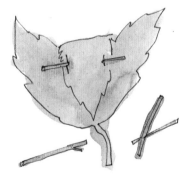

2 Fold the center point forward, then thread a thin twig through it. The ends of the stick make the fox's eyes.

15

Leaf crown

1 Collect lots of big leaves that have interesting shapes and colors. Use strong autumn leaves, or press fresh young leaves for one to two weeks.

2 Design the crown by arranging the dried leaves on a sheet of thin cardboard. Pick a big leaf for the center.

3 With a pencil, lightly trace around the leaves so that you know how much of the cardboard they cover. The leaves should actually be a little bit bigger than the cardboard.

4 Take the leaves off the cardboard. Cut out the shape just inside of the pencil marks so that the cardboard will be completely covered by the leaves.

5 Glue the leaves onto the cardboard, laying the smaller ones on top of the big one. Add some leaves with long stems as extra decoration.

6 Cut out a strip of thicker cardboard about 1 in (2½ cm) wide. Hold the strip around your head and tape the ends together. You might need an adult to help you do this. Tape the band to the crown and decorate the band with small leaves.

Daisy chains

Pick some common garden daisies, making sure that you leave a long stem on them. Make a short split in the stem with the nail of your little finger. Thread the stem of another daisy through the split. Repeat the process until the chain is long enough to go over your head. Make a long split in the stem of the last daisy and thread the head of the first daisy through it so that it acts like a lock.

Leaf mask

1 Paint the underside of some leaves with a paintbrush.

2 Lay the painted sides down on white paper.

3 Place a second piece of paper over the top and press down. Make sure that each entire leaf makes contact with the bottom sheet of paper.

4 Very carefully remove the top piece of paper and the leaves. Let the printed shapes dry.

5 Cut out a mask shape from paper. Hold it up to your face and carefully mark where your eyes are. Remove it from your face and cut out eye holes.

6 Cut out some of the printed leaves. Arrange them into a shape for your mask.

7 Glue the leaf prints onto the mask shape making sure you don't cover up the eye holes.

8 Carefully make small holes at the edges of the mask. Thread through two pieces of string or ribbon so you can attach the mask to your face.

19

Decorated curtain

1 Ask an adult to help you measure the window, then cut a piece of muslin to fit it.

2 Fold the muslin in half lengthwise to find the center. Mark it with a stick pin. Fold each of the halves in half again lengthwise and put in two more pins. Repeat, putting in a pin marker each time. Trim the curtain if you would like a neat edge, or leave it ragged.

Naming the plants

If you know the names of all the plants, you can write them on the curtain with a special fabric pen. White muslin can be bought inexpensively from most fabric stores and it makes a pretty decorated curtain. Muslin is best, but very thin white cotton also works well. You do not have to cover a whole window—a narrow strip looks good, too.

20

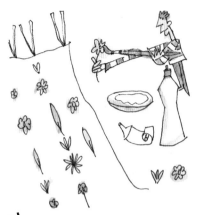

3 Count the pins in the muslin and cut that many lengths of ribbon, fabric tape or strips of fabric. Make the strips about 10 in (25½ cm) long. Fold them in half to find the center, then sew the center of the strips onto the muslin at the points marked by the pins. Take the pins out.

4 Lay the muslin on a clean floor or large table. Arrange your collection of pressed leaves and flowers in a pattern on the curtain.

5 When you are happy with the design, gently apply a dot of glue to the back of each flower or leaf and pat them onto the curtain. Let dry.

Dandelion pompon

6 Ask an adult to hang the curtain up at the window. Use the fabric strips to tie the curtain to a rod or to a piece of string pinned across the window frame.

1 Pick a dandelion flower that has not opened.

2 Tie a piece of cotton thread around the top of the flower.

3 Carefully pull the flower away from its stem and hang it up.

4 As the flower dries out, it will open out into a pompon.

Lampshade

1 Ask an adult to take a plain-colored shade off a lamp. Wrap a sheet of white or light-colored paper around the lampshade. Use two sheets of paper taped together if necessary.

2 If there is excess paper, make light pencil marks on the inside of the paper, outlining the top and bottom of the shade.

3 Open up the paper and cut out the shade shape.

4 Attach pressed flowers and leaves to the paper shade with tiny dots of glue.

5 Ask an adult to put the shade back on the lamp, and slip the pressed-leaf cover over it. Switch on the light to see the outlines of the flowers and leaves.

Decorated candles

1 Gather together some smaller pressed leaves and flowers, then choose a candle.

2 Spread thin craft glue onto the backs of the leaves and flowers. Wait until the glue has become "tacky" before sticking them to the candle. If the flowers are very fragile, spread the glue on the candle and gently pat the flowers onto it.

Stain pictures

1 Draw a plant or flower in pencil. You could draw flowers growing in your garden, or gathered in a vase.

2 Rub the leaves and petals of actual flowers onto the drawing to color in the picture. Red petals give the most vibrant color and pollen gives a strong yellow color.

Bark rubbing

Hold a piece of paper against the trunk of a tree. Rub crayons over the surface of the paper to pick up the texture of the trunk. You can also do this by placing paper over wall plaques and church brasses.

Leaf windows

1 Use two sheets of clear glass from clip frames. Make sure the glass is clean.

2 Put insulating tape on all four sides of one sheet of glass. Make sure that half of the tape sticks out beyond the edge of the glass. Lay the glass down with the tape sticky side up.

Once the season changes, you can find other interesting leaves and flowers. To change your leaf exhibit, simply untape and replace. If you want to make a larger exhibit, use two sheets of hard, clear plastic instead of glass. Always be careful when handling glass.

3 Arrange some pressed leaves and flowers on the glass. Spread them out evenly. Leave space between the leaves so that the sunlight can shine through.

4 Lay the other sheet of glass on top, being careful not to move the leaves. Fold the tape up and press it onto the glass.

5 Place the frame on a windowsill. Leaves will fade if the sun is too strong, so do not put it where the sun is too bright.

25

Chocolate rose leaves

You can use the leaves of any scented rose, but first wash them thoroughly by soaking them in water for half an hour.

1 Ask an adult to help you melt some chocolate. Place it in a pan inside a larger pan that has boiling water in it.

1 Collect some leaves with nice shapes. Take a sheet of photographic paper out of its sealed bag.

2 Put the paper in a sunny spot and quickly arrange the leaves on top of it. Leave them there until the paper starts to change color.

Transpiration

2 When the chocolate has melted, lay clean rose leaves face down on a sheet of wax paper. Using a new paintbrush, paint a thick layer of chocolate onto the leaves.

3 When you remove the leaves, you will see silhouettes that will slowly fade away.

3 Place the leaves in the refrigerator for about half an hour until the chocolate has hardened. Carefully peel off the rose leaves and use the chocolate leaves to decorate cakes or to give as a present.

In a process called "transpiration," water is sucked up through the stem of the plant into the leaves and petals. To see how this happens, fill two glasses with water. Add food coloring to one of them and stir well. Choose a white flower with a strong stem and slice the stem in half lengthwise. Stop about halfway up and put some tape around the top end of the cut to stop the stem from splitting any further. Put each half in a separate glass. The food dye will be drawn up the stem and start to color half of the petals within one hour.

Ice bowl

1 Find two bowls that are almost the same size as each other. Rub a little margarine on the inside of the bigger bowl and some on the outside of the smaller one.

2 Drop a few small rose petals and mint leaves into the bigger bowl. You can use any edible leaves and flowers, but make sure that they are clean.

Flower ice cubes

3 Pour cold water into the bigger bowl until it reaches about a third of the way up. Now put the other bowl inside it so that the water is sandwiched between the two. Put the bowls in the freezer and leave for about five hours or overnight until frozen.

1 Put clean rose petals, mint leaves, and other edible flowers—violas, small pansies, borage flowers, nasturtiums, chickweed—into an ice cube tray and fill it with water.

2 Place the tray in the freezer and leave for two to three hours or until the cubes are frozen solid. Use them to chill cold drinks.

4 Take the bowls out of the freezer and when the ice is just beginning to thaw, pull the bowls apart gently to reveal the ice bowl. Wipe off the grease, put the ice bowl on a plate and fill it with fruit.

29

Fancy frames

I nstead of keeping your favorite drawings and photographs locked in a drawer, show them off in these fun frames. Stand them on a table or ask an adult to hang them up on a wall.

Beechnut frame

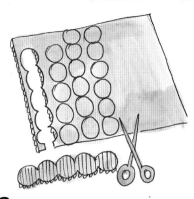

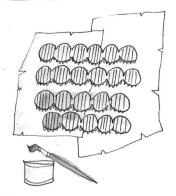

1 Lay a strip of corrugated cardboard flat side up. Trace the bottom of an egg cup onto it. Move the egg cup and draw around it again, making sure that the edges of each circle touch.

2 For a square frame, trace four lines of connecting circles all the same length. For a rectangular frame, make two of the lines longer. Make four strips and cut out.

3 Turn the strips of cardboard corrugated side up and paint them. Gold paint looks good, but any color will do. Let dry.

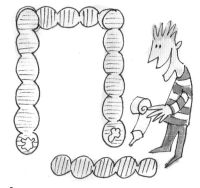

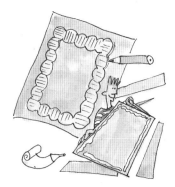

4 Lay the strips out in the shape of a frame and glue the two end circles of each line to the end circles of two other strips. Let dry.

5 Lay the frame on a piece of cardboard and trace around the curved edges. Cut the cardboard just inside the line and glue the frame to it. Let dry.

6 Decorate the frame with beechnuts. When they have fallen and opened up to let their seeds out, they look like little bells. If you cannot find these, use acorns or dried leaves, or make flower shapes from fruit seeds.

7 Cut a picture or photograph into a shape that fits into the center of the frame. Carefully dot a little glue around the edges of the picture and place it in the frame.

8 To make the frame free-standing, cut out a strip of thick cardboard that is wider at the bottom than at the top. Tape the top to the back of the frame and bend it out to make a support.

Nature Facts

The biggest seeds in the world are coconuts, which can weigh over 33 pounds (15 kg)! Coconut palms often grow along the seashore and their seeds are carried away by the waves.

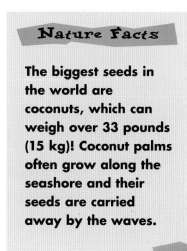

31

Leaf frame

1 Collect some colorful autumn leaves and arrange them in a frame shape on a piece of thick cardboard. Make a mark where the inside edge of the frame will be. Take the leaves off and cut out the middle of the cardboard. Decide how wide you would like the frame to be by holding the leaves against it.

2 Carefully glue one leaf at a time onto the long sides, overlapping them as you go. Keep the stems pointing inwards.

3 When the long sides are covered, stick leaves on the short edges. Glue a big leaf in the center, top and bottom.

4 Glue some leaves on top of others to make an interesting pattern. Use contrasting colors and shapes for the best effect. Let dry.

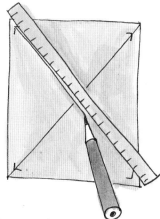

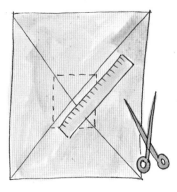

5 Lay the frame on a piece of thick cardboard and make four marks at each inside corner. Remove the frame and use a ruler to draw a line from one mark to another. Cut the cardboard about ¾ in (2 cm) outside the lines so it will fit behind the frame.

6 Use a ruler to draw two diagonal lines from each corner of the cardboard to its opposite corner to find the center.

7 Decide how big you want the picture hole to be. Make four marks on the four lines that are the same distance from the center. Connect the marks, then cut out the hole.

8 Cover the cardboard with brown paper. When dry, turn the cardboard over and snip through the paper where the hole is. Cut from the middle to the corners, fold the paper through the hole, and tape it down.

9 Lay the leaf frame face down, being careful not to break the leaves. Spread the glue about ¾ in (2 cm) in from the outside edge of the cardboard, then lay it on top of the leaf frame.

10 Tape the photograph or picture behind the hole and tape a piece of thick string, yarn or twine to the back of the frame so that you can hang it up.

Pine cone frame

1 Ask an adult to straighten out a wire hanger, then twist it into a circle. If you do not have a hanger, use thick wire. It should be about 2 to 2 ½ ft (12 to 18 in) long.

2 Using soft, malleable wire, attach the pine cones to the heavy wire circle. Hold each cone against the wire circle and tightly wind the wire around it.

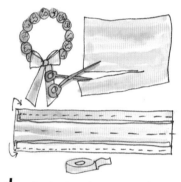

4 Make the bow by cutting a long strip of fabric about 4 ¾ in (12 cm) wide. Fold in the cut edges of the fabric and tape them down with double-sided tape. Tie the bow onto the wire circle to fill in the gap.

6 Turn the frame over and first glue and then tape the tabs to the edge of the circle. Tie string to the top of the frame at both corners to hang it up.

Driftwood frame

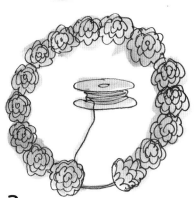

3 Keep doing this until you have gone all the way around the circle. Push the cones tightly together to make a space at the bottom for the bow.

1 Lay four pieces of driftwood on cardboard. Mark the outside corners of the frame. Connect them with straight lines. Cut out and paint the cardboard. When dry, turn it over and trace around the picture you want to frame. Cut a hole just smaller than the picture.

2 Tape the picture to the back of the frame. Turn it over and glue the driftwood around the edges.

5 Lay the frame over a piece of thick cardboard and mark where the inside of the frame is. Remove the frame and draw a face on the cardboard. Draw four rectangular "tabs." Then cut out the face with the tabs.

3 Glue shells around the frame. Attach a piece of soft wire, twine or thin roping to the back with heavy tape so that you can hang it up.

You can find interesting pieces of driftwood washed up on a beach or along a river bank. Make sure that they are clean and free of insects before taking them home.

Nature Facts

Animals that make shells are called mollusks. The shell is their home and it also protects them from enemies. When collecting shells on a beach, make sure they are empty, otherwise the creature that lives inside could die.

Plant pots and vases

Don't throw away empty plastic bottles and other containers—turn them into colorful vases and plant holders.

Papier-mâché head

1 Blow up a balloon—you might need the help of an adult to inflate it completely. Cover it in three or four layers of papier-mâché and let dry overnight, then apply three or four more layers.

2 Cut off the top of the papier-mâché shape and any hanging pieces of balloon left over.

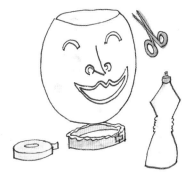

3 Cut out a triangle from cardboard, fold it in half and tape it to the middle of the face to make a nose.

4 Roll up thin strips of newspaper and tape them to the face to make nostrils, eyebrows and lips. Apply papier-mâché over them and the nose. Let dry.

5 To make a stand for the head, cut a strip of thick cardboard, bend it around the bottom of the head and tape it into a ring. Glue it to the bottom of the head. Place a weight inside the head so the join between the head and stand is secure. Let dry.

How to make papier-mâché

To make papier-mâché, tear sheets of newspaper into small pieces. Mix some flour and water together until the paste is as thick as a very thick milkshake. Drench the newspaper pieces in the flour and water paste, then apply in layers. Let dry for 12 hours before applying more.

6 Paint the face. When it is dry, glue on paper eyes and teeth, and make eyelashes from black paper. Cut a plastic bottle in half and place it inside the head.

7 Fill the container with water and fresh flowers. Or, to give the head "hair" that grows, use the container for a plant that has lots of trailing leaves.

37

Papier-mâché ladybug

1 Apply papier-mâché to a balloon. When dry, cut the shape in half lengthwise. On one half draw the head, the wings and a black stripe along the body with a marker. Draw a triangle on the wider end of the body and cut it out.

To make the ladybug, you need only one half of a papier-mâché balloon. Use the other half to make a second ladybug or another insect.

2 Paint the body of the ladybug red and the face black. While the paint is drying, cut out two cardboard egg cartons for the eyes and paint them white. When they are dry, add black pupils.

3 Paint big black spots on both wings.

4 Collect six thick twigs about 3 in (7½ cm) long and paint them black. Let dry.

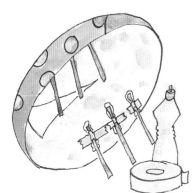

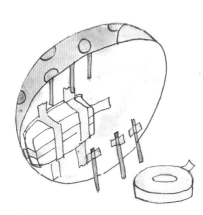

5 Use glue and tape to stick the twigs securely to the inside of the body to make legs. Make sure the length of the sticks that fall below the body are just about even, or else the ladybug won't balance.

6 Tape a plastic container inside the ladybug, directly under the triangular hole. This is where the flowers will go.

7 Paint two twigs black. While they are drying, glue the eyes to the body and add white highlights to the pupils. Make two small holes in the ladybug's head and push the twigs through them to make antennae.

Snail watching

To see how a snail moves, gently pick one up and put it in a glass bowl. Watch it from underneath as it moves across the glass. When you have finished, make sure you put the snail back and clean the bowl!

Flower truck

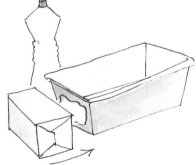

1 Lightly sandpaper a plastic container and spray it with hair spray—this will help the paint stick to the plastic. Paint the container and let dry.

2 To make the cab of the truck, turn a small box inside out. Stick it back together, plain side out, using double-sided tape. Paint it and let dry.

3 Glue the cab to the body of the truck and leave it somewhere safe to dry.

Funny face vase

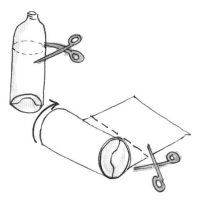

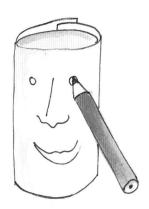

4 To make wheels, cut two small tubes in half. You will need three of the halves. Draw around the end of one tube on cardboard, cut out six circles, and glue them over the ends to seal them.

1 Cut off the top of a plastic bottle. Roll a sheet of paper around the bottle and mark where it overlaps slightly. Cut it to size.

2 Hold the paper against the bottle and lightly mark where the eyes, nose and mouth will be with a pencil.

Even if you have only a tiny plot of land, you can grow lovely flowers for your home. Plant the seeds in clusters, planting tall plants behind smaller ones.

5 Tape and glue the wheels securely to the underside of the truck.

3 Draw and color in the face, then fasten the paper around the vase with a strip of tape down the back.

6 Draw two squares for side windows and an oblong shape for the front window. Draw the driver and a passenger, cut them out and stick them to the cab. Now the truck is ready to be filled with flowers.

41

Spring basket

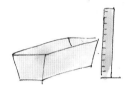

1 Wrap string around a plastic container to find out how long a sheet of colored paper you will need. With a ruler, draw about seven strips that long and ½ in (1¼ cm) wide. Cut along the strips, almost to the end of the paper.

2 Find a sheet of different colored paper that is as wide as the first one. Measure the container and make the paper that high plus ¾ in (2 cm). Draw strips that are about ½ in (1¼ cm) wide and cut them out.

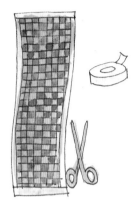

3 Tape the uncut end of the long strips to a table top, then weave the short strips into it. The first short strip goes under, then over, then under again. The second strip goes over, then under. Repeat.

4 Once each short strip has been weaved into the long strips, tape the uncut end to the edge of the last long strip so that they do not come undone. Make sure that the tape will not show on the right side.

5 Stick double-sided tape to the back of the woven strip and wrap it around the container, leaving a flap of about ¾ in (2 cm) at the bottom. Turn it upside down, snip the corners and tape the paper to the bottom.

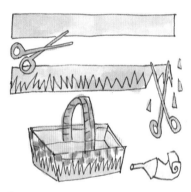

6 Cut a strip of cardboard long enough and wide enough to make a handle. Weave some more colored paper, wrap it around the cardboard strip and stick it down with double-sided tape. Tape the handle inside the container.

7 Cut a strip of green paper (or plain paper painted green). Snip V shapes in it along one edge and glue it to the basket so it looks like grass.

8 To decorate the basket, draw, color and cut out garden creatures like butterflies, bees and worms, and glue them in position.

43

Twig toys

Build a village hut, design your own miniature courtyard, and make a horse and rider using twigs, soil and other natural ingredients from your collection. You will need a strong forked branch to make the striped catapult on page 56.

Bird's nest

1 Collect six long, curved twigs and cut them so that they are all about 12 in (30½ cm) long. Choose twigs from a willow or vinka vine. They will be the most flexible.

2 Lay each twig at a different diagonal, one over another, so the middle of the sticks form a thick center. Tie them firmly together in the middle. This is the basic frame for the nest.

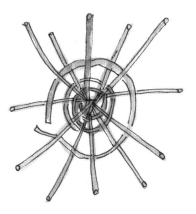

3 Weave in other long, soft twigs. Begin close to the center, weaving the twigs over and under the frame. Push the twigs down toward the center as you go around.

4 As you add additional twigs, gradually pull up the twigs that form the frame to make the sides of the nest.

5 When you have worked your way up to the top of the nest, fill in the gaps by weaving in straw and grass. When the nest is complete, cut off the string.

Nature Facts

Birds build their nests out of all kinds of material, including hair and scraps of paper. If you find an old, empty nest, look more closely at how it was made. Before you handle a nest, make sure that it is not still in use. Many birds raise more than one family in a nest and return to it year after year.

Usually the breeding place has plenty of food, but only for a short time, so the birds have to migrate once their eggs have hatched. Not all birds migrate by flying. Emperor penguins swim and walk up to 370 miles (600 kilometers) across the Antarctic ice to reach their breeding grounds.

Eggshell birds

1 Carefully pierce a fresh egg at the top and bottom with a needle.

2 Blow very hard into the hole at the narrow end of the egg. If nothing comes out, make the hole at the bottom slightly bigger. Blow the egg into a bowl.

If you can find a goose egg, you can make a really big bird!

3 Fill a cup with water, take a mouthful, then blow the water into the egg. Gently shake the egg, then blow the water out into a bowl. Now the egg will be clean inside. Let dry.

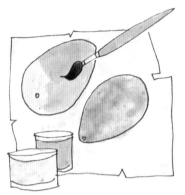

4 Paint the egg and let dry.

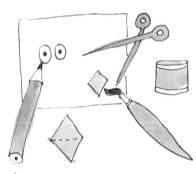

5 Draw two eyes on white paper and cut them out. Color a small piece of paper yellow. When it has dried, cut out a yellow diamond. Fold this in half to make a beak.

6 Glue the eyes and the beak to the narrow end of the egg. Push some feathers into the hole at the fat end to make a tail. Glue a feather to each side of the egg for wings.

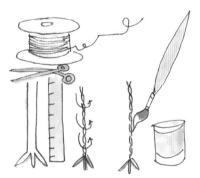

7 Cut two pieces of soft wire that are just more than twice as long as you want the legs to be. Bend each piece in half and make a claw. Twist the rest into legs. Paint yellow and let dry.

8 Carefully make two small holes in the bird's belly with a needle and push in the legs. Arrange them so that the bird will stand up.

Twig horse

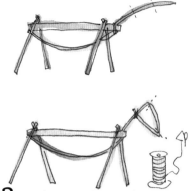

1 To make the horse's legs, cut four twigs about 6 in (15 cm) long. Bind each pair into a V shape using soft, malleable wire or string. For the body and neck of the horse, choose a thicker twig with a long, soft stem. Place the legs over the twig and bind them with soft wire.

2 Attach a curved twig with wire to make the belly and bend the twig back on itself to make the head.

3 Attach a Y-shaped twig to the head for the ears. Bind it with wire.

4 Collect some very small twigs and make them into a tail by binding the ends with wire and wiring the bundle to the body.

Twig rider

1 Collect six twigs about 7 in (18 cm) long. They should be a little flexible so that they do not break when bent. Gather them into a bundle and bind them at the top and around the middle with soft, malleable wire.

2 From the middle of the bundle to its bottom, split the bundle into two groups of three twigs each and bind the ends with wire. Now the figure has a body and legs.

3 To make arms, take two forked twigs and bind them to the top of the body.

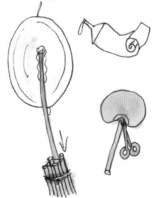

4 To make feet, take two more forked twigs and push them into the ends of the legs. If necessary, wind some more wire around the ankles.

5 To make a head and a neck, make a hole in an acorn and push a twig into it.

6 Push the neck into the middle of the body and glue a feather to the head.

Twig star

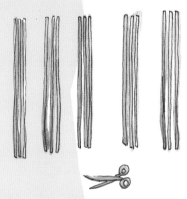

1 Collect 15 twigs about 6 in (15 cm) long. Divide them into five groups of three.

2 Bind two of the groups together with string to make a V shape. Bind another two groups so that you have two V's.

3 Lay one V across the other and tie the left end of one over the right end of the other.

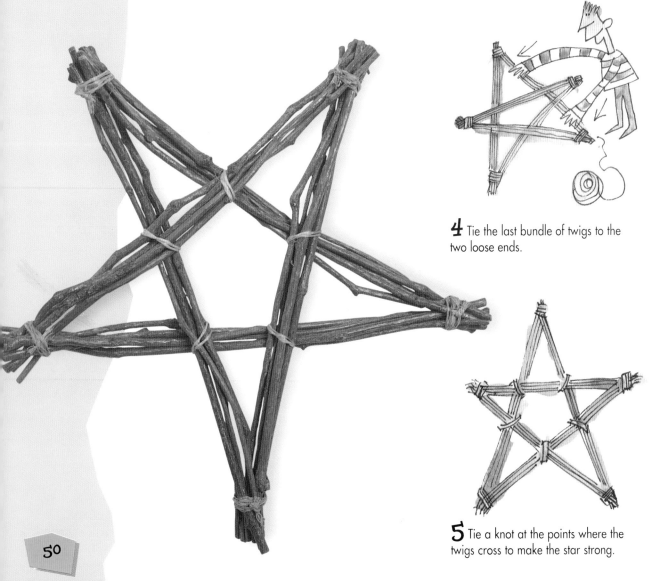

4 Tie the last bundle of twigs to the two loose ends.

5 Tie a knot at the points where the twigs cross to make the star strong.

Drawing with twigs and feathers

You can use all kinds of sticks, grasses and feathers to draw with.

1 Cut feathers at different angles to make interesting brush marks.

2 Use forked twigs or tape twigs together to draw many lines at once.

Village hut

1 Collect some dried grass or straw, or buy some from a pet store.

2 Cut out a strip of newspaper about 14 in (35½ cm) long and 5 in (13 cm) wide.

6 On a piece of thick cardboard, draw a curved shape for the hut to stand on. Cut it out and glue the hut to it.

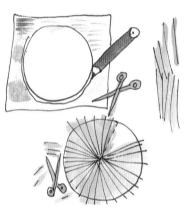

3 Cut enough straw to cover the strip of newspaper. Spread a layer of glue on the paper, then stick the straw on it. Leave the end bare. Trim off any loose ends of straw.

4 Spread glue on the bare end of the paper, then wrap the other end around and press the ends together. When the glue has dried, cut a doorway in the hut.

5 Trace a plate onto newspaper and cut out the shape. Make a cut in one side of the circle up to the middle. Glue straw to the circle so that it spreads out from the center like a star. Leave a clear area near the cut.

7 Spread craft glue on the bare area of the circle, fold it under and stick it down to make a cone-shaped roof. Put it on the hut. Mix water and soil with a little craft glue and spread the mixture over the base and around the hut.

> If you make lots of huts, you can have your own village. Color and cut out wild animals to place between the huts.

53

Mini courtyard

You can cut out people and garden furniture from magazines, glue them to cardboard, and place them in the yard.

1 Use a tray, a shallow baking pan or a low-sided box as the garden base. Line it with aluminum foil.

2 Draw your courtyard design on a sheet of paper. Will it have a patio, trees or a swimming pool?

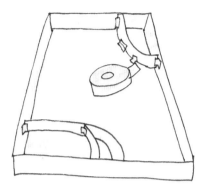

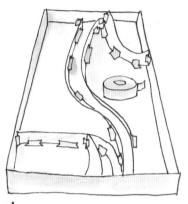

3 Collect lots of ingredients such as soil, pebbles, moss, twigs, sand and dried flowers to make the courtyard. Keep them in jelly jars or plastic bags.

4 Begin by building up flower beds. Cut some strips of cardboard and tape them to the tray.

5 Tape thin strips of cardboard into the base to make the edges of a path.

6 Make a lawn from moss or cut grass. Line the path with gravel, sand or pebbles. Use twigs for trees, and add a shallow container lined with foil for the swimming pool.

7 To make a clothesline, tie some string to two twigs. Cut out clothes from magazines and glue these to the line. Push the posts into the soil, or tape them to the edge of the tray.

Nature Facts

Plants need sunlight to make their food. They can't live if they don't get enough. You can see how important sunlight is by moving lawn furniture or a wood pile on your grass lawn. Uncovering the grass beneath, you will see that it is yellow and unhealthy looking. But wait! Now that you have exposed it to the sun, the grass will slowly recover and soon turn green.

Snails love gardens. See page 121 for some interesting snail facts.

Catapult

1 Find a strong, forked branch. If you can't break off the ends, ask an adult to cut a branch into a Y shape for you.

2 Paint it a pale color, then prop it up to dry. When dry, paint dark stripes on it.

3 Tie some dressmaker's elastic tightly across the V shape of the Y.

Practice firing scrunched up balls of paper into a wastepaper basket or at a target.

Teasel mouse

1 Draw and cut out two cardboard ears and glue them into a teasel head. Glue on two cloves for eyes and a berry for the nose.

2 Cut a strip of fabric 2 ft (61 cm) long and 3½ in (9 cm) wide. Thread a needle with cotton, tie a knot in the end and do a long running stitch along one of the two long edges. Pull the cotton through so that the fabric scrunches. Join the two sides and make a knot stitch at the end to stop the skirt from coming undone.

3 Bend the stem of the teasel down and stick it through the hole. If the teasel does not have a stem, make one from a strip of cardboard.

If you cannot find a teasel, use a small pine cone instead.

4 Cut a hole on each side of the skirt and thread a slim stick through for arms.

5 Arrange the skirt so that the mouse stands up.

Nature pictures

Twig forest

1 Glue dried twigs and leaves to a piece of thin cardboard. Arrange them to look like a forest.

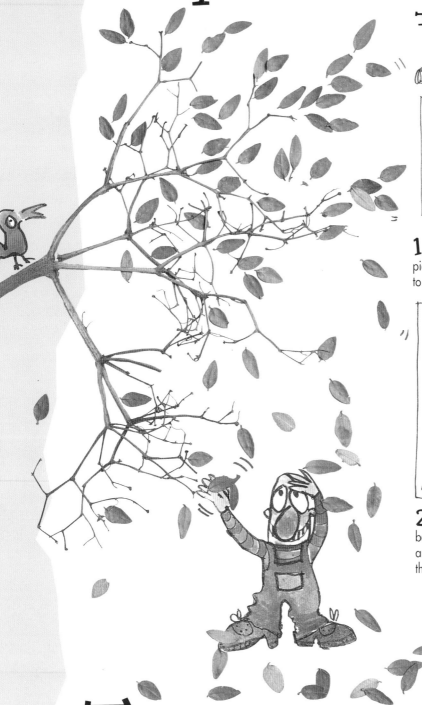

2 Draw animals and birds hiding between the trees. You can also color and cut out more figures and glue them to the twigs.

The next time that it rains and you can't play outdoors, turn your collection of twigs, pebbles, shells and other bits and pieces into colorful pictures. Dried beans and pasta shapes are also good collage ingredients.

58

Country house

1 Lay out all the things that you have collected on walks—twigs, leaves, feathers, pebbles, nuts, seeds, flowers—and think about a collage you can make with them. Sketch the scene on a sheet of thin cardboard.

2 Paint in a pale sky, then spread a layer of glue over the bottom part of the paper. Sprinkle soil or sand over it to make the ground. When the glue has dried, shake off the excess.

3 Build up the rest of the picture. Cut twigs to make a fence, use bark for buildings, cut feathers into V's for birds, use twigs and flowers for the garden and nuts for animal heads. Use plenty of glue to stick everything in place.

1 Save the shells from eggs. Wash them out and let dry. Draw a face with hair and shoulders in profile on a sheet of thick paper. Spread glue over the face and neck, then squash the eggshells onto it, the darker sides of the eggshells up.

2 Fill any gaps with small bits of shell and let dry. Now cut out the profile.

3 Glue lines of beans and seeds of pod bearing plants (peas and beans) onto the shoulders to make a striped shirt. Spread glue between the lines and sprinkle on lentils to fill the gaps. When the glue has dried, shake off.

4 Paint a piece of thick cardboard as a background for the portrait. Make sure that it is big enough for the head and shoulders. When dry, glue the profile to the cardboard.

5 Make hair by gluing corn silk, dried pasta, bark or coconut fiber to the head.

6 Make a necklace from sunflower seeds, glue on a bean for an eye, decorate the hair with small pine cones, and stick pressed flowers to the background.

Use all sorts of things collected from walks or found in the kitchen to make this woman.

Nature Facts

Around the world, people have adapted to their environments. The Bedouin of the Sahara have learned to cope with scorching heat during the day and bitter cold at night. The people of northern Canada have adapted to life surrounded by snow and ice all year long.

Weather projects

Weather vane

1 Collect four sticks, three the same length and one a bit longer. If you can't find four straight sticks, use bamboo stakes.

2 Bind two of the shorter sticks together with string to make an X. Tie this to the long stick about 4 in (10 cm) down from its top. Use lots of string to make it strong.

Whether you live in the country or in the middle of a busy city, you can make these projects that use the wind and the sun.

3 Draw, color and cut out an N for North, S for South, E for East and W for West from a piece of cardboard.

4 Glue these to the ends of the cross and hold them in place with clothespins until dry. Make sure you get the letters in the right order!

5 Find an old plastic ball-point pen and make sure its stopper is in the bottom. Remove the refill and ask an adult to cut the empty pen in half. Bind the bottom half to the top of the weather vane, open end of the empty pen up.

Bamboo stakes can be purchased at garden centers and hardware stores.

6 Draw and cut a tail plate out of cardboard for the wind to blow against. Make a smaller cardboard figure for the pointer at the other end. Glue these to the ends of the stick and hold them in place with clothespins until dry.

7 To find the center of the indicator stick, balance it on your finger until it stays perfectly straight. Mark the spot. Cut a piece of wire three times as long as the attached half of the ball-point pen. Fold the wire in half over the stick where the mark is, and twist the ends together.

8 Slide the wire into the pen so that the indicator can turn freely. First check that you have N in the right position with a compass, and then place the weather vane in a windy spot.

Hula dancer wind chime

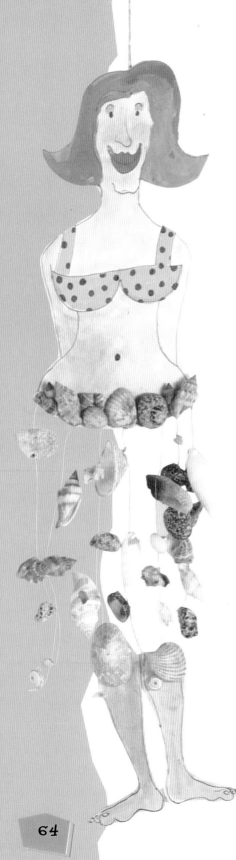

1 Draw the top half of the hula dancer on a piece of thick cardboard. Color her in and, when dry, cut her out. Look at the body and decide how long you would like the skirt to be, then cut about six pieces of strong, clear plastic wire to that length plus 1¾ in (4½ cm).

2 Gather together lots of different shells. Some may already have holes in them, but ask an adult to make a hole in the others with a thick needle. Knot the shells onto the pieces of plastic thread, leaving a small gap between each shell.

Windmill

1 Cut out a piece of thin cardboard 7 in (18 cm) square. Draw diagonal lines from one corner to the other, then cut along the lines leaving about ½ in (1¼ cm) uncut at the center.

2 Cut out a star from a piece of colored paper and push a stick pin through its center. Bend the corners of the cardboard into the middle and tape them down in the center to keep them from reopening. Thread the pin through the center of the windmill so that the windmill can rotate. Decorate the windmill.

> Hang wind chimes in a doorway or by a window where the breeze can move them. You can use all kinds of things—as long as they rattle! Collect pieces of old pottery, beads and nutshells. Tie string around large, heavy pieces of pottery.

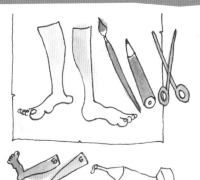

3 Along the dancer's tummy, carefully make six holes for the wires. Thread the wires through the holes. To keep them from passing through the tiny holes, knot the plastic wires. Around those knots, knot a piece of twine so the threads can't slip out.

4 Draw and color two lower legs for the dancer. When they are dry, cut them out and glue them to the ends of the two middle wires.

5 Decorate the dancer's waist and knees with some more shells. Tape a length of string to the back of her head and hang her in a breezy spot so the shells rattle.

3 Paint a straight stick or bamboo stake. When it is dry, glue a strip of thick cardboard to one end.

4 Thread a tiny bead over the end of the pin. Cut a thick slice off the end of a cork, then carefully push the pin through the cardboard and into the cork.

Nature Facts

Sea breezes are made from heat and air. As the sun warms the land on a hot day, the air above it is warmed, too. This warm air rises, and cooler air flows in from the sea to take its place. At night, the land cools down but the sea remains warm, so the wind blows in the opposite direction. That's why it is often windy by the sea.

Sundial

1 Open out a corrugated cardboard box. Draw around a large plate and cut it out. This will be the face of the sundial.

Here are the Roman numerals for 1 to 12: I for 1; II for 2; III for 3; IV for 4; V for 5; VI for 6; VII for 7; VIII for 8; IX for 9; X for 10; XI for 11; XII for 12.

66

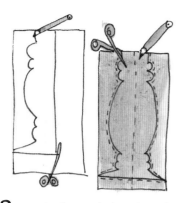

2 To make the stand, draw the outline of half a leg on a sheet of paper and cut it out. Trace around the shape on the piece of cardboard. Flip the pattern over and trace around it again to make the other half of the leg. Cut it out. Copy this to make a second leg.

3 Paint both sides of the legs and the circle, waiting for one side to dry before painting the other side.

4 When the paint has dried, cut a slot halfway down from the top to the middle of one leg, and halfway up from the bottom and to the middle of the other. Make the slot as thick as the thickness of the cardboard. Slot the legs together to make a stand.

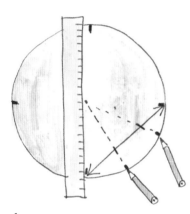

1 = I
2 = II
3 = III
4 = IV
5 = V
6 = VI
7 = VII
8 = VIII
9 = IX
10 = X
11 = XI
12 = XII

5 Use a ruler to find the center of the circle and mark off the quarters. Putting the ruler between 3 o'clock and 6 o'clock, divide the quarter into three. Mark where 4 and 5 o'clock will go.

6 Write Roman numerals on the clock face. Cut out a cardboard triangle that is as long as the distance from the middle of the clock face to the numbers and half as high as the distance from the middle of the clock face to the numbers. Glue the triangle to the clock face so that the pointed end faces XII.

7 Place the clock face onto the stand and put it in a sunny garden facing southeast. As the sun moves across the sky from east to west, the pointer will cast a shadow on the sundial, telling you what time it is.

Cork raft

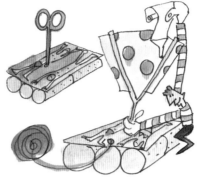

1 Collect six bottle corks and lay them together in two rows on a piece of cardboard. Draw a rectangle around them, then cut it out. Glue the corks onto the cardboard and let dry.

2 Find a sheet of colored paper. Trace around the raft, then cut out the paper and glue it to the cardboard deck. Draw and color some sunbathers, cut them out and glue them to the raft.

3 Carefully make a hole in the middle of the raft with the closed blade tip of a pair of scissors. Make a sail by cutting a triangle of cotton cloth and gluing it to a forked twig. Push the mast into the raft between two corks. Secure a string to the raft so that you can pull it along.

Nature Facts

Rain provides all the water we use in our homes. Rain seeps down through the ground and in certain places, such as hill slopes, the water reaches the surface and seeps out as a stream. That stream will merge with other streams, or tributaries, and grow into a river. Some river water is collected in reservoirs and then pumped through pipes to treatment centers to be filtered before reaching our homes.

Paper boats

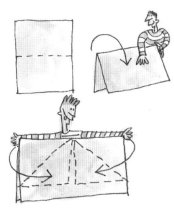

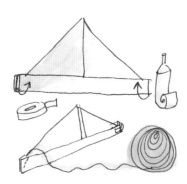

1 Fold a rectangle of paper in half lengthwise. Then, from the folded edge, fold in both corners, leaving a wide margin at the bottom.

2 Fold up the open, bottom edges twice on each side of the boat. Glue a length of string to one end of your boat so that you can pull it along in the water. Tuck the ends in securely, or tape them down.

3 You can paint people directly onto your boat or cut out people from a magazine and glue them on.

Pooh sticks

Christopher Robin and Winnie the Pooh played this game in a story by A. A. Milne. Choose twigs that are about the same weight, but make sure that you can tell whose is whose. Stand on the upstream side of a bridge and drop the twigs in the water. Run to the other side of the bridge to see which twig floats by first. The fastest is the winner.

Perfect presents

Lavender snake

The right sides are those that will show in your finished project. The wrong sides are those that you do not want to see.

1 Draw the curving outline of a snake on the right side of a piece of fabric. Cut it out.

2 Turn the snake pattern over, pin it to the right side of a different colored piece of fabric, and cut out a second shape.

Everyone likes to receive presents, and homemade ones are extra special. In this section, you will find ideas for scented gifts, necklaces and decorations.

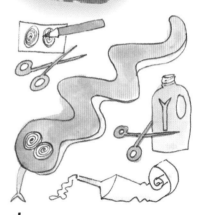

3 Keeping the right sides of the fabric together, sew around the edge of the snake but keep the head open. Turn the snake inside out and stuff it with cotton and sprigs of lavender.

4 Make a tongue out of bright colored plastic or painted cardboard. Glue it inside the mouth, then stitch or glue the head closed. Draw two eyes on cardboard, cut them out and glue them to the snake's head.

Potpourri in a coconut bowl

1 Carefully make two holes in a coconut and drain out the milk. Ask an adult to cut the coconut in half, then take out the coconut flesh.

2 Wash the inside of the coconut, then use sandpaper to smooth the outside. Use furniture polish to make the coconut bowl shiny.

3 Chop up and mix together lots of fragrant dried herbs such as rosemary and bay leaves. Add fresh lavender, cloves, dried flower heads, rose petals and various powdered spices.

4 Make orange peel shapes to decorate the potpourri. Take off large pieces of peel from oranges and tangerines. Carefully cut out stars, hearts and other shapes, then let them dry on an open shelf or a very sunny windowsill. Alternatively, you can place them in the oven at the lowest setting for half an hour.

Scented angel

1 Find a piece of fabric about 5½ in (14 cm) wide and 3½ in (9 cm) long. Fold it in half widthwise, right sides together, and cut out a head shape. Sew the long, curved edge of the head together. Turn the head right side out and fill it with cotton and sprigs of lavender.

2 Fold another piece of fabric in half, wrong sides together, and cut out the shape of the gown. Glue a long stick across the wrong side of one piece of fabric for the arms, and two sticks for the legs.

4 Glue peppercorns to the face to make eyes, a nose and a mouth. Use dried flowers for the hair.

6 Make a loop from a piece of ribbon and glue it to the back of the angel. Hang it by your bed, or use it to scent towels in the bathroom.

Pomander

3 Sprinkle on lavender flowers. Glue the head to the body. Spread glue on the edges of the stick figure and stick the other piece of fabric on top, right side up.

1 Choose a firm, round orange. Push cloves into the orange in a line from top to bottom. Make three more lines so that the orange is divided into quarters.

5 Carefully glue two pressed leaves to the back of the angel so that they look like wings. Decorate the gown with pressed flowers.

2 Keep making lines of cloves until the orange is covered. Place the orange in the oven at the lowest setting for half an hour so that it will dry out completely. Tie a ribbon around the orange and use it to scent your closet.

Hundreds of years ago, the Greeks and Romans used lavender because they liked its fresh, clean smell. A few drops of lavender oil added to your bath will make the water smell good and feel soothing.

Lavender soap

1 Grate about 5 oz (125 g) of unperfumed soap. This is a good way to use up old pieces of soap.

2 Place two or three big handfuls of lavender in a teapot or bowl and ask an adult to pour in two cups of boiling water. Stir the mixture around and let it brew for a few minutes.

3 Pour some cold water into a saucepan, then place a smaller pan in it. The water level should reach halfway up the side of the smaller pan.

4 Place the larger pan on the stove. Pour the grated soap and a little of the lavender water into the small pan.

5 Heat slowly until the soap has melted. Add more of the lavender water if necessary.

Orange and cinnamon soap

To make orange and cinnamon soap, add the peel from two grated oranges and two teaspoons of cinnamon powder to plain water instead of lavender water.

6 Remove both pans from the heat. Add about three tablespoons of oatmeal to the soap mixture and stir well.

7 Grease two small molds or cookie cutters with margarine or petroleum jelly and place them on a sheet of wax paper.

8 Carefully spoon in the soap mixture and smooth down the top with the back of a hot spoon. Run the spoon under hot water to keep it warm. Let the soap dry—this can take up to a week.

9 When the soaps are dry, take them out of their molds and leave them for a month in a dry place on some tissue paper.

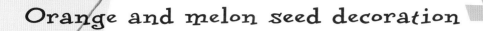

Orange and melon seed decoration

As well as cutting an orange into slices, you can make cuts in the sides of a whole orange. These oranges will take longer to dry out than the slices.

Mini star

1 Carefully cut an orange into thin slices. You may need the help of an adult to do this.

1 Cut six twigs to the same length. Be careful handling the scissors.

2 Tie the ends of two twigs together very tightly with string to make a V shape. Tie a third twig across the ends of the V shape to make a triangle. Repeat with the other three twigs so that you have two triangles.

2 Lay the slices on a sheet of wax paper and dry them on a warm shelf or a very sunny windowsill. Alternatively, place them in the oven at the lowest setting for half an hour.

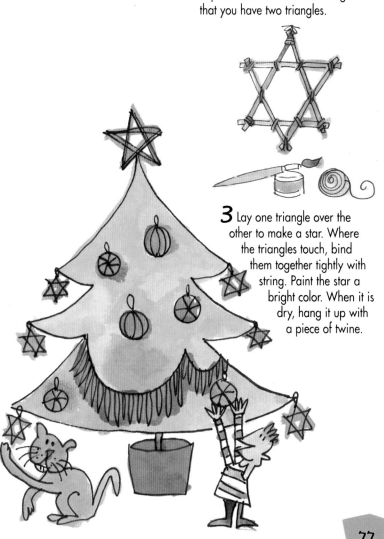

3 Lay one triangle over the other to make a star. Where the triangles touch, bind them together tightly with string. Paint the star a bright color. When it is dry, hang it up with a piece of twine.

3 Save the seeds from a melon. Wash them, spread them out to dry and then paint them. When dry, thread the seeds with the orange slices onto a piece of string.

Sunflower seed necklace

1 Once a sunflower head has gone to seed and started to dry, harvest the seeds to make a pretty necklace.

2 Thread a length of nylon string onto a thin needle and carefully push the sunflower seeds onto it, one by one. Push the needle through the fat end of the seed, from edge to edge. Keep your fingers out of the way!

Chili and bayleaf decoration

3 Tie two lengths of nylon to the ends of the necklace so that you can tie it around your neck. If you have the clasps from an old necklace, sew these to the ends of the string.

1 Pick chilies from a chili plant or buy them fresh from a store. Thread a length of strong nylon string onto a needle. Put on some rubber gloves. Carefully push the chilies onto the needle, one by one. Keep your fingers out of the way!

2 Thread some bay leaves onto the string—they look good with the bright red chilies. When complete, hang them up in the kitchen to decorate the room.

Nature Facts

Sunflowers were brought to Europe in the sixteenth century. The Spanish conquistadors brought them back from Mexico, where they had been grown for 3,000 years. Sunflower seeds are full of vitamins and are good to eat without their striped outer shells. The thick stem is used to make many things, including paper and textiles.

3 Rinse your gloves. Adults can use the chilies to cook spicy dishes. Remind them to wear gloves and to wash their hands well after handling the chilies because they can burn.

Fruit and vegetables

Funny animals

1 Look at the shape of the vegetables and imagine what animals they could be. Pick large vegetables for the bodies.

You can make all kinds of things from fruit and vegetables. Turn a potato into a funny face, or make an apple-faced woman. Only use fruit and vegetables that no one is planning to eat!

5 Attach a long nose in the same way as the legs. Use half toothpicks pushed through the front of the nose to make two black nostrils.

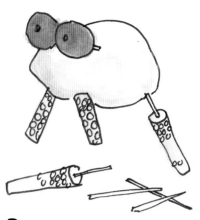

2 Slices of radishes, carrots or scallions, and whole peas or beans make good eyes. Spike the eyes from behind onto toothpicks. If you like, use green olives with pimentos for pupils.

3 Spike the legs lengthwise with a toothpick and stick these into the body. Use rhubarb, sticks of celery, small carrots or baby corn for a big animal. For a spider, use eight beans.

4 Spike the tail lengthwise and attach it like the legs. For a big animal, use asparagus or scallions. Use a leafy piece of celery to create a bushy tail.

Nature Facts

When is a vegetable not a vegetable? When it is a fruit, a flower or a root! A fruit is the part of the plant that contains the seeds, so although we call green beans, eggplants and peas vegetables, they are really fruit. Cauliflower and broccoli are really flowers, and carrots, parsnips and radishes are roots.

6 Pin on a smiley mouth made from a stem, or use a knife to cut a zig-zag in the head and form teeth.

7 Ears can be made from half a pea pod, or vegetable leaves. Cut slices from a big potato for elephant ears.

8 Carve scales, spots or stripes onto the bodies. Use tomato stalks for eyelashes and toothpicks for whiskers.

81

Apple-faced woman

1 Peel an apple. Then carefully cut away the sides and the top to make a face shape. Cut a big smiling mouth, a nose and two holes for eyes.

2 Pour salt into a jelly jar. The salt should be about 1 in (2½ cm) deep. Add 4 in (10 cm) of hot water and stir until the salt dissolves. Leave the apple face in the jar overnight. This will preserve the apple and keep it from molding.

5 Cut off excess fabric, leaving a margin of ½ in (1¼ cm) of fabric around the cardboard shape. Fold over the fabric edges and glue to the body. Glue apple face and stick to the body.

Potato prints

3 Take out the apple face and let it dry. Make a hole in the bottom of the apple and insert a strong stick. Push in two cloves for eyes.

1 Choose a large potato and clean it. Carefully cut the potato in half and pat it dry with a paper towel.

2 Using a pencil, draw an outline of the shape you would like to print on the cut surface of the potato. You can have a different pattern on each half. Simple shapes work best.

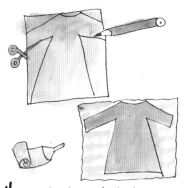

To make animal paw prints, copy the shapes cats and dogs leave with their muddy paws!

4 Draw the shape of a body on cardboard and cut it out. Glue the pattern onto the wrong side of a piece of fabric. The wrong side is the side you do not want to show. Let dry.

6 Cut a triangle of fabric and tie this around the head like a scarf. Glue leaves or twigs to the ends of the arms for hands.

3 Carefully cut away the area that you do not want to print. Cut around the shape and then out to the sides so that the pieces come out. You may need to ask an adult for help with this.

4 Pat the surface dry again, then brush on some paint. Press the potato gently onto the paper so that it will not smudge.

Potato faces

1 Draw noses, eyes, mouths, mustaches, hair and ears on the back of an empty cereal box or a piece of thin cardboard.

2 Paint the features and let them dry. Cut them out. Choose some large potatoes for heads.

3 Slice the bottom off each potato so that it will stand up. Carefully attach the noses, mouths and other features with stick pins.

1 Carefully slice off the side of a lemon.

2 Cut this slice in half lengthwise, and cut off the ends.

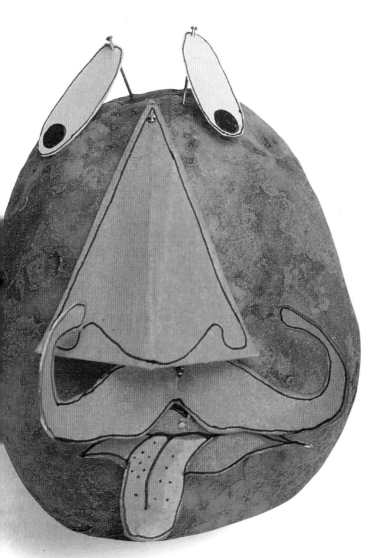

3 Use two toothpicks to attach the ears. Push in cloves for eyes, a nose, and the tail.

Other stuff

> Cattails grow wild in rivers and on river banks. They can also be bought from florists. If you can't find one, use a long pine cone instead to make the body, and glue the eyes and feathers onto it.

If you have a cattail or a pine cone, you can make a bird mobile to hang over your bed. Here are some more ideas for toys to make from odds and ends.

Cattail bird

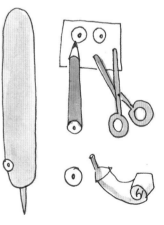

1 Cut the top part of a cattail off its stem. Paint the tip of the cattail yellow.

2 Draw two small eyes on white paper and make the pupils black. Cut them out and glue them on either side of the cattail.

Grass whistle

3 Dip the quill end of a feather into glue and push it into the end of the cattail to make a tail feather. Add a few more to make it bushy.

1 Find some strong, thick blades of fresh grass. Pick a piece that is longer than your thumb.

2 Hold the blade of grass tightly between your thumbs and blow on it very hard to make a whistling sound.

4 Dip the quill ends of two more feathers into glue and stick them into the side of the cattail for wings.

Pinhole camera

1 Find a clean, empty tin can with a lid.

2 Carefully make a hole in the side with a hammer and nail. You may need the help of an adult for this.

5 Tie a piece of elastic around the middle of the bird so that it bounces. Ask an adult to pin the other end of the elastic to the ceiling.

3 Take the lid off the can and insert a piece of photographic paper, cut to fit. Put the lid back on and point the hole toward a nice view. After about five minutes, take out the paper to reveal a ghostly image of the scene.

As soon as you take photographic paper out of its sealed bag it will start to turn black, so you must put it in the can really quickly. The image you make with the pinhole camera will gradually fade away.

Grass doll

1 Pick a big bundle of very long, fresh grass.

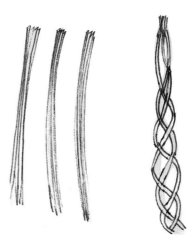

5 Make three groups of a few strands of grass each. Twist the three groups together at one end two or three times. This will keep the grass from unbraiding. To braid, fold the right-hand strands over the center, then the left-hand ones over the center, and continue until you have nearly run out of grass. Twist the ends securely together.

Place the doll somewhere warm to dry. When dry, she will be very fragile, so be careful.

2 Use a small pine cone as the base for the head. Lay the cone in the middle of a big handful of grass. Fold the grass over the cone lengthwise. Twist the grass at the bottom of the cone to make the neck.

3 Twist a few strands of grass together and tie them around the neck two or three times. Twist the ends around the back and tuck them in to keep them from coming apart.

4 Get a handful of grass and fold it around the shoulders to make a shawl. Cross it over the front of the body and tie it at the waist with some more strands of grass twisted together at the doll's back.

6 Twist the braided grass into a ring that fits around the head. Cut it to the right length and twist the ends together.

7 Make two more braids for arms and tie the ends with some strands of grass. Turn the doll around and push the arms carefully under the shawl at the back. Make a gap for the arms with a pencil. Spread out the grass at the end of the arms to look like hands.

8 Trim the bottom of the skirt to neaten it. Push three sticks under the skirt so that the figure can stand up. Make sure it balances by placing the sticks equal distances from one another in a triangle shape.

Nature Facts

Because plants cannot move, they have developed lots of ways to disperse their seeds. Grass seeds are light and can be carried by the wind. Sycamore seeds have "wings" that help them to spin away from the tree.

Indian headdress

1 Open out a large corrugated cardboard box. Draw the headdress on the corrugated side with the ridges going top to bottom. Make sure that the space for your face is the right size.

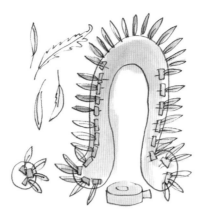

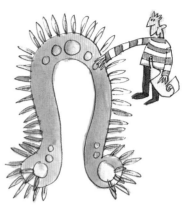

2 Paint the headdress and cut out and color some shapes for extra decoration. Let dry.

3 Push small feathers into the holes at the top of the cardboard and tape big ones to the back of the headdress.

4 Glue the colored shapes onto the front of the headdress.

5 Cut out a strip of thick cardboard about 1 in (2½ cm) wide. Hold the strip around your head and tape the ends together. You might need an adult to help you do this. Remove the band and tape it to the back of the headdress.

Nature Facts

For birds, feathers are a vital overcoat that holds in their body's heat. Dinosaurs were the ancestors of birds, and their feathers developed from the scales of dinosaurs. Feathers are made from keratin, which is the same material that forms human skin, nails and hair. Each feather is made up of tiny strands of keratin attached to a central quill. Even though they are very light, a bird's total weight of feathers can be twice as heavy as its skeleton.

1 Make a bed of modeling clay or play clay about 1½ in (4 cm) thick. Build up a wall about 2 in (5 cm) thick, joining it securely at the base.

2 Press the object you want to copy about halfway into the bed, being careful not to mark it with your fingers. Pull it out so that an impression is left in the clay.

To make plaster casts of animals'
paw prints, pour the plaster into the
paw shape. When the plaster has
set, lift the cast out and wash it with
warm water.

3 Pour two cups of water into an old
container. Shake in about three cups
of plaster, or enough to form a peak
that sticks out of the water. Mix it into
a paste as thick as glue.

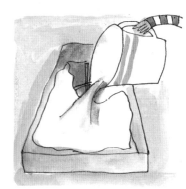

4 Pour the plaster into the mold so
that it seeps into the imprint and
covers it completely. Let it set for about
15 minutes.

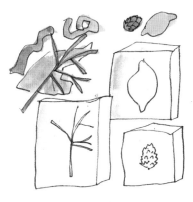

5 When the plaster has dried, pull
away the clay. Carefully wash your
new plaster cast.

Growing things

In this section you can plant a hanging basket, watch an acorn grow into a tiny oak tree, or make a head with long green hair!

What you will need:

Potting soil
Peat moss
Gravel or pebbles
Sand
Sawdust
Seeds and flowers
Small plants
Root vegetables
Plant pots
Blotting paper
Plastic containers
Pair of tights
Paint can
Fruit crate or basket
Heavy plastic bag

How to feed your plants

Plants need nitrogen in order to grow, and one of the best ways to provide them with this food is by mixing compost into the soil. To make compost, save kitchen waste such as vegetable peelings, leaves, eggshells and tea bags. If you have a garden, layer the compost with grass cuttings and plant clippings. If you do not have a garden, keep the waste outside in a plastic bag. Eventually the compost will rot and, when mixed into soil, will provide your plants with the nutrients they need.

How to grow plants from fruit seeds

If you have a sunny windowsill, you can grow all kinds of plants from fruit seeds. The seeds from oranges, lemons, apples, cherries, peaches and melons will all grow into new plants. Soak the seeds overnight in a jar filled with water and then let them dry. Fill a small plant pot with soil and water it. Make a hole ½ in (1.5 cm) deep with your finger or the eraser end of a pencil. Drop the seed in the hole and gently fill up the hole with soil. Do not pat the soil down hard, or water it too much. If the soil is too wet or packed down, oxygen will not be able to get to the seed and it will die. Cover the pot with brown paper and keep it in a warm, dark place for a few weeks. When shoots appear, move the uncovered pots to a sunny spot.

Tips

Peat is a useful plant food. It is the remains of plants that were broken down thousands of years ago in wet, marshy conditions. You can buy peat, as well as potting soil, in bags from garden centers.

Store gravel, stones and broken pieces of slate and pottery in plastic bags. Put these odds and ends in plant pots before you add the soil. By partly covering the holes at the bottom, they will help water to drain out, but keep the soil in.

You can decorate plant pots to make them look nicer. If they are plastic, first rub them lightly with sandpaper so that the paint will stick to the surface. Be careful not to spill water on the pot because the paint will run.

Miniature gardens

Each seed contains a
baby plant that needs
only moisture,
warmth and light to
grow. Most plants
shed their seeds in the
autumn. During the
winter, they lie in the
ground. When spring
comes, they burst into
action, plunging their
roots into the soil and
sending shoots up into
the air.

1 Find a recently fallen acorn. Fold up
some toilet paper or a paper towel
and place it at the bottom of a clean
jelly jar. Dampen the paper by misting
or sprinkling it with a little water.

4 When the acorn has sprouted,
gently remove it from the jar and throw
away the paper. Fill the jar with water
and tape a piece of clear plastic over
the top of the jar.

You do not need lots of room to have your own
garden—you can grow a jungle on a plate! And
there are lots of things that you can grow for free
by sprouting the seeds of fully grown plants,
like acorns.

96

2 Take the cap off the acorn and lay the acorn on the damp paper.

3 Place the jar on a sunny windowsill and keep the paper moist by misting or sprinkling a few drops of water on it.

Growing an avocado

You can sprout an avocado pit by balancing it over a container filled with water. Keep the bottom of the pit in the water until roots appear. When the roots are thick and strong, plant the avocado in potting soil.

5 Cut a slit in the plastic and carefully thread the acorn shoot through the slit so that it reaches the water and the acorn sits on top of the plastic.

6 Keep the water level high enough to cover the shoot and watch the acorn grow leaves. When the roots are big enough, plant the acorn in potting soil.

97

Jack and the Beanstalk

1 Wash out a jelly jar and soak off the label in warm water. Let dry.

3 Glue Jack to the outside of the jar. Cut a piece of blotting paper long enough to fit snugly inside the jar.

5 Paint a long stick that the bean can climb up. While the paint is drying, draw, color and cut out a castle in the clouds. Glue it to the end of the stick.

Bean racing

Plant two beans in separate jars and see which one reaches the castle first.

2 Draw Jack on some thin cardboard, color him in and cut him out.

4 Poke a bean down between the paper and the jar next to Jack. Keep the absorbent blotting paper damp by adding water to the jar.

6 When the bean has sprouted, tape the stick to the outside of the jar. As the bean grows, wind it around the stick so that it will eventually reach the castle.

Blotting paper can be purchased at stationery and office supply stores.

Egg heads

1 Break the small end of an egg with the back of a spoon. Wash it out and let dry.

2 Draw a funny face on the shell with a pencil or felt-tip pen.

3 Use paint or felt-tip pens to color in the details.

Nature Facts

Lots of the fruit and vegetables we buy in supermarkets have been grown using artificial fertilizers and pesticides. These are powerful chemicals that destroy pests, such as greenflies, but which also kill butterflies, bees, ladybugs and other "friendly" creatures. Organic farmers use only natural methods to discourage insect pests and weeds. They fertilize the land by recycling household waste like peelings and eggshells.

4 Use a cup from an egg carton or a strip of cardboard to form the body. Decorate it.

5 Carefully fill the eggshell with cotton balls and place the shell on the body.

6 Sprinkle in some cress or mustard seeds. Use a small jug to water them, being careful not to spill any on the face.

7 Put the cress heads in the dark. When you see tiny shoots appear, move heads to a sunny spot and watch the hair grow.

Grass head

1 Cut off the foot from a pair of old nylons. Pour in a little sawdust and tie it off with string to make a round nose.

2 Pour in more sawdust and add some grass seeds. Then top off with more sawdust. Keep the grass seeds at the top of the head, otherwise the man will have a hairy face!

3 When the nylon is full enough to look like a head, tie it off with a knot.

After a week, the grass head will have long green hair. If you cut the grass, in another week it will grow back again. This is because the "growth point" of grass is at ground level. The cress in the egg heads also grows quickly. The narrow stems have pairs of green seed-leaves at the top. When you cut off these seed-leaves, the cress will stop growing because the growth point of cress is in the seed-leaves at the top of the stem.

4 Find a small plastic container or cut off the base of a plastic bottle. Place the head in the container. Cut a strip of paper long and wide enough to cover the container and paint the paper to look like a striped shirt. Tape it around the container. Cut another piece to look like a collar, then cut out a bow tie. Glue them to the shirt.

5 Cut out two eyes from plastic and use a waterproof pen to draw the pupils. Pour some water into the container—it will soak through the sawdust to the grass seeds. Fill the container with water daily and the head will grow green hair!

Nature Facts

A "weed" is any kind of flower growing in the wrong place. Many gardeners call wildflowers weeds because they don't want them in their gardens. Some gardeners use chemicals called weedkillers to destroy the plants they don't like.

1 Find a very large glass jar with an opening big enough for your hand and wash it out well. A large pickle jar should be big enough. Let dry.

2 Put some gravel and a layer of sand in the bottom for drainage.

3 Add some peat moss so that the jar is about half full, then put in some small plants.

4 Draw animals, monsters or people on thin cardboard, color them and cut them out.

5 Cut strips from a plastic bottle and glue them to the cardboard figures. Now you can push them into the soil without the cardboard getting soggy.

Strawberry tower

Choose three or four plant pots of different sizes and fill each of them with soil. Build a tower, placing the widest pot at the bottom and the smallest at the top. Plant young strawberries in the gaps around the pots. Place the tower in a sunny spot and keep the soil damp. As the plants grow, they will trail down the sides of the tower.

Mini greenhouse

Young potted plants will love this greenhouse, too.

1 Soak the label off a large, clear plastic bottle, then carefully cut the bottle in half around the middle and keep the top.

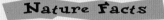

Nature Facts

Plants grow faster in a greenhouse because the sun's rays pass through the glass and heat up the air inside. To see this effect for yourself, place a glass jar over a patch of grass or seeds growing in a tray. The plants inside the "greenhouse" will grow more quickly than those outside. Like the glass container, the earth's atmosphere is a shell that traps the sun. The gases that create the shell let the sun's warming rays in, but not out!

2 Paint a terra cotta or plastic plant pot in bright colors. If the pot is plastic, prepare it first by sandpapering it lightly so that the paint will stick.

3 When the pot is dry, lay some pebbles or pieces of rock in the bottom. This will help water to drain out of the pot, but will keep the peat moss in.

4 Fill the pot with peat and plant some seeds. Slip the top half of the bottle over the pot. Put the mini greenhouse in a sunny spot and keep the peat moist. If it gets too wet, take off the bottle top and it will dry out.

Vegetable top jungle

1 Ask an adult to keep the tops of root vegetables—such as carrots and parsnips—when chopping them up. The top part is where the leaves sprout.

2 On a saucer or small plate, lay the vegetable tops on blotting paper. Add a little water and place them on a sunny windowsill. Keep them damp and soon they will sprout new leaves.

3 Make some animals for the jungle. Draw monkeys, elephants and other wild animals on thin cardboard and color them in. Cut them out and tape a strip of cardboard to the back so they can stand among the leaves.

Hanging basket

1 Find a paint can. If there is any paint left in it, you can pour it into a wide-necked jar and use it in step 3. Or pour it onto thick layers of newspaper. Fold these up and put them into the trash. Wash out the can and let dry.

3 Paint the can. Paint the top few inches inside, too. When the can has dried, turn it upside down and paint the bottom. Let dry.

The filled pot will be heavy, so ask an adult to hang it on a post or bracket for you.

5 Lay some pebbles or pieces of slate in the bottom. This will help water to drain out of the pot. Fill it with peat moss, then add the plants.

6 Tie some strong string or twine around the handle of the pot so you can hang it up. If there is no handle, ask an adult to make one by tying twine around the lip of the can. Pull one end over and tie it to the other side.

Window box

2 Very carefully, use a hammer and nail to punch drainage holes in the bottom. Ask an adult for help with this.

1 Get a fruit crate from your local grocery store or a plain basket and paint it a basic color. Paint the top few inches inside, too. Let dry.

2 Draw flowers on the side with a pencil, then color them in with poster paint and let dry.

4 Poke a nail through any holes that have been blocked with paint. Turn the can right side up and paint a pattern on it with enamel paint. Let dry.

3 Line the crate with a strong plastic liner—cut it down if it is too big. Make a few small holes for drainage. Lay pebbles and pieces of rock at the bottom, then fill the crate with soil. Plant vinka vine and flowers, and remember to keep the soil damp.

Wildlife

N

o matter where you are, you can spot wildlife if you know where to look. Read on, and you will find out how to tempt birds and butterflies to your garden.

What you will need:

Sand
Soil
Plants
Coconut
Nuts or seeds
Sticks
Twigs
Dried and fresh flowers and leaves
Glass tank
Clear plastic frames
Insulating tape
Coins
Paper bags
Teacup candles
Taper or long match
Plastic sheeting

How to prepare jelly jars for the teacup candles

1 Soak the jelly jar in warm water until the glue softens, then peel off the label and throw it away. Let the jar dry. To make a handle, tie string around the neck of the jar, then pull one end of the string over and tie it to the other side.

2 Cut a sheet of paper that is as high as the side of the jelly jar and long enough to go around. Use this method for the tissue paper, face, bat, and pressed flower lights.

How to spot wildlife

What kinds of wildlife can you see in your garden or from your window? A fragrant wildflower garden will attract butterflies, bees and insects. You can attract birds by putting out nuts and seeds. To study them, sit very still—any movement might frighten the birds away. If you have a pair of binoculars, you can look more closely at the birds' markings. If you are lucky, squirrels and other small mammals might pay you a visit, too.

Tips

Insects like to hide under leaves and behind loose bark. Use a magnifying glass, if you have one, to see the creatures in more detail. If you carefully lift the corner of a log or a pile of wood you might uncover hibernating animals as well as insects. Check holes in fences for scraps of fur. Look out for animal tracks in snow or damp ground.

If you have to pick up a small animal or insect to study it, be very gentle. Pick up very small creatures, such as caterpillars, with a leaf, spoon or a new paintbrush. Study them for a little while, then return them to where you found them.

Before you add goldfish to a pond (page 135), let the fish float in a plastic container full of water on the surface of the pond for an hour. This will help them adjust to the water temperature. Feed the fish in cold weather. In the summer, they will eat larvae and insects that fall in the water.

Jar lights

Decorated jars containing flickering teacup candles look lovely placed outdoors on a warm evening. But don't use them indoors, and always have an adult light them for you!

Funny face light

 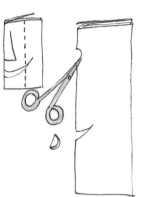 

1 Fold a sheet of paper in half. Cut out half a mouth along the folded edge. On the same edge, snip a short and a long line to make half a nose.

2 Fold the paper again at the edge of the mouth and cut out a semi-circle for the eyes.

3 Unfold the paper to reveal a smiling face. Stick colored tissue paper behind the eyes and mouth. Make hair by snipping another piece of paper and gluing it to the back of the paper before you tape it around the jar.

Spotted light

Bat light

 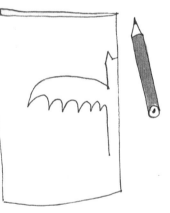 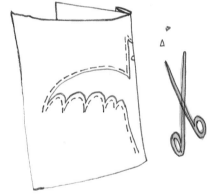

1 Make a polka dotted jelly jar by tearing holes in the paper before you glue it down the back seam. Stick small pieces of colored tissue paper in the gaps. You can use the shapes you tore out of the first piece to decorate another jar.

1 Fold the paper in half and draw the outline of half a bat along the folded edge. Leave a gap at the bottom of the paper.

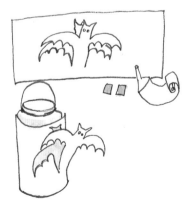

2 Fold the paper again along the face and cut a small hole in the folded edge. This will make the eyes. Cut around the bat shape from the head down, leaving the body attached at the bottom.

3 Glue red tissue paper behind the bat's eyes, then wrap the paper around the jar and tape it down the back seam. Pull the bat away from the jar so it looks like he's flying.

Moths are attracted to electric lights and candles in the same way that they are attracted by the light of the moon, by which they navigate.

Cut paper lantern

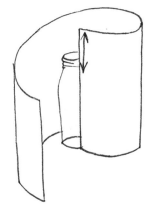

1 Cut a piece of paper that is long enough to go around a large jelly jar, but half as tall again.

2 Fold the paper in half lengthwise. Cut interesting shapes into the folded edge, leaving about 1 in (2½ cm) uncut.

Pressed flower and leaf light

1 Arrange pressed flowers and leaves on the paper and, when you are happy with the design, use a little glue to stick them in place. Wrap the paper around the jar and tape it down the back seam.

The best plants to pick are those with very colorful flowers that the light will shine through, or dark leaves with a nice shape.

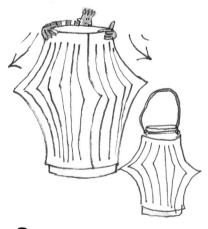

3 Unfold the paper. Wrap it around the jar and fasten it to the base with clear tape. Push the paper down from the top so the slots open out, and tape it around the top of the jar.

Striped light

1 To make a striped light, measure a sheet of tissue paper and stick it to the jar by gluing it down the back seam. Then tear long strips of a different colored tissue paper and wrap them around the jar, using tiny dots of glue to stick them to the back.

115

Paper bag lights

1 Collect strong white or brown paper bags. Draw on them with felt-tip pens, leaving the bottom inch clear.

2 Pour enough sand, very dry soil or grains of rice into the bag to make it stand up securely.

3 Place a teacup candle inside the bag. **Do not** use any other kind of candle.

4 Spread out the sand in the bag so that the candle is not close to the sides. Ask an adult to light it with a long taper or match.

Stained glass lights

1 Fold a piece of paper like an accordion and cut different shapes in the edges. Make some big and some small. Unfold the paper and if there are areas without holes, fold it up again and make some more.

2 Unfold the paper. Cut out small sheets of colored tissue paper and glue these over the holes, using a small brush to apply dots of glue around the edges of the holes.

3 When all of the holes are covered, wrap the paper around the jar—gluey side down—and tape it along the back seam.

117

Insects and birds

Birds and small creatures can be just as much fun to watch as bigger animals. Play with the caterpillar playground and the racetrack outdoors in case the insects try to escape!

Wormery

1 Start by laying coarse material, such as pieces of slate or gravel, at the bottom of the container. This aids drainage.

2 Add sand and soil in alternate layers to make the wormery look nice. End with a layer of soil.

3 Plant a small plant in the back of the wormery. Be careful not to disturb the layers by digging too deep.

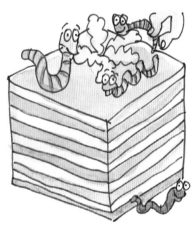

4 Lay the earthworms on top and cover them with some leaves. The worms will drag these leaves into the soil and eat them.

5 Keep the wormery in a dark place —worms don't like bright light—and keep the soil moist. Watch the worms create channels as they burrow through the sand and soil.

Nature Facts

Earthworms keep the land healthy by burrowing through the soil, making tunnels that rain water and air can pass through to nourish the roots of plants below. Plants and trees need minerals in order to thrive and grow. As plants and animals perish they form "humus." Humus contains the minerals that plants need. Worms pull these minerals down from the surface of the earth and into the soil, where the roots of the plants feed.

Spiders and snails

Different spiders build different kinds of webs, but the web you are most likely to see is the vertical orb-web. Below, you can see how the female spider spins her web (adult males don't spin webs). Snails, however, don't need to build homes because they carry them on their backs. They like to hide in cool, damp places.

Spider's web

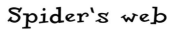

1 Make a bridge between two twigs by letting out a fine strand of silk. Strengthen this first thread by going over it again, then spin another to hang loosely below it.

2 Drop down from the middle of the loop until you find an anchoring place. A leaf will do. The three points of this Y-shaped frame are the first spokes in the web.

4 When the framework is complete, make a small spiral at the center to lock the spokes in position.

5 Spin a temporary, non-sticky spiral from the center to the edge of the web.

do not have shells, they are covered with sticky slime to keep them damp. The slime also tastes bad, which stops most birds from eating them.

● Snails can live for up to ten years, but they have lots of enemies—including gardeners. Slugs and snails like to eat young, tender plants, but we shouldn't try to get rid of them with poisonous chemicals. Poison can kill other animals as well, and a bird that eats a poisoned snail will be poisoned, too.

● You can study snails by tracking them. Hold the snail gently by the shell and draw a number on it with water-based paint that won't harm the snail. (Make sure you do not get any paint on the snail's body.) Put a large clay flowerpot upside down in the garden and prop up one edge. Early the next morning, remove any snails from the pot, make a note of their number and then put them back. Do the same snails return the following night? How often do new ones appear?

Snail facts

● The biggest land snail in the world is the giant African snail. Its body can grow to be over 8 in (20 cm) long! The Japanese brought the snail to the Pacific area during the Second World War as a source of fresh food. At the end of the war, American troops accidentally took some live snails back to the United States.

● The snail's shell helps prevent the snail from drying out. Because slugs

3 When the long thread is firmly attached to a leaf, spin some more threads between the branches and from the edge of the framework. Take them into the center of the Y.

6 Turn around and work your way back into the center, gathering up the temporary spiral and laying a sticky spiral in its place. The web is now ready to catch flying insects.

Spiders are very clever. To stop themselves from becoming stuck in their own webs, they produce an oily substance and cover their legs with it!

121

Insect racetrack

1 Open out a cardboard box and cut off one of the large sides. This will be the base of the racetrack.

2 To make sides for the track, cut two strips of cardboard as long as the base and two as wide. Make them all about 2 in (5 cm) wide. Lay a strip of tape under one edge of the base with half of the tape sticking out. Place a strip of cardboard on the tape and fold it up. Use smaller pieces of tape to make the corners.

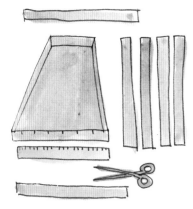

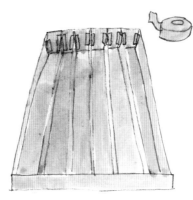

3 Divide the width of the box by about 1½ in (4 cm) and make marks where the lane dividers should go. Cut strips of cardboard 2 in (5 cm) wide and as long as the track.

4 Tape the lane dividers in place.

5 To make a starting gate, cut a strip of cardboard a little wider than the racetrack. Cut out a rectangle for each of the lanes. Make them as wide as each track and twice as deep.

6 Slot each rectangle in a lane at the end of the box, then tape their tops to the long strip of cardboard.

7 Paint the box and the starting gate and let them dry.

8 Slot the starting gate back in the track and place the insects in position. When you are ready to start the race, lift the starting gate and they're off!

123

Caterpillar playground

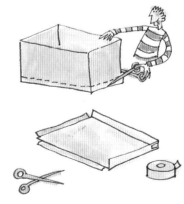

1 Cut the bottom off a cardboard box, leaving the sides about 2 in (5 cm) high. If you cannot find a box with a flat bottom, cut off one of the long sides of a box. Cut four strips for the sides and tape them together.

2 Paint the playground inside and out. Let dry.

Don't forget to put the caterpillars back where they came from after playing with them.

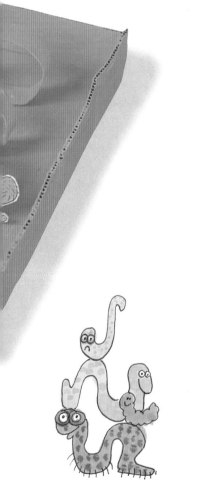

3 Collect four sticks of the same length and one a little longer. Tape the four short sticks into two V's and tape the long stick under them.

4 Cut two sticks to the same length for the ladder. Glue twigs or toothpicks across them for rungs.

5 Lay down a sheet of newspaper and paint the monkey bars and the ladder. Let them dry.

6 Cut a toilet-tissue tube into sections and paint them. Let dry.

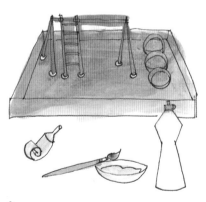

7 Glue the monkey bars, ladder and hoops into the playground base.

8 Make a trapeze from a twig and two pieces of string. Tie another piece of string between the frame and the corner of the box. Add small twigs and fresh leaves and the playground is ready for play!

Ant town

126

1 Use two sheets of glass from clip frames that are the same size. Cut three strips of thick cardboard—two the same height as the glass, and one the same length. Make them about 1 in (2½ cm) thick.

2 Cover the strips of cardboard with insulating tape so that the damp sand will not make the cardboard soggy.

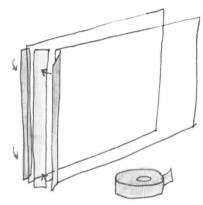

3 Attach the covered cardboard to the edges of the glass with more insulating tape. When you have finished, you will have a narrow tank.

4 Fill the tank with clean sand—use layers of different colored sand if you have it. If not, add layers of clean soil in between the sand. Leave a big gap at the top of the tank for the houses.

5 Now make a lid that will fit snugly over the tank. Cut one more strip of cardboard that is as long and as wide as the top of the tank. Cut two that are as long but a little narrower. Cut two small pieces for the ends. Tape them all together.

Catch ants for the ant town by letting them crawl up a stick. Feed them with bread crumbs, dead insects or flies. Make sure that you keep the sand slightly damp.

6 Cut a piece of thin cardboard as long as the tank and slightly deeper than the gap between the top of the tank and the sand. Draw a row of buildings or trees and color them in. Leave a clear strip at the bottom. Cut out the scene and put some tape along the bottom to keep it from getting soggy.

7 Dampen the sand and push the cardboard strip into it. Put the lid on and make some tiny air holes in it with a pin. Make some holes in the surface of the sand, then put in some ants and watch them make passageways through the sand.

Balancing butterfly

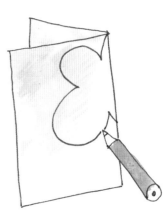

1 Fold a sheet of paper in half. Draw half a butterfly, making sure that the bottom wing is bigger and wider than the top wing. The bottom wing should hang lower than the body so that the butterfly can balance.

Moths and butterflies have a fine powder on their wings that helps them to fly. You should never pick up butterflies by their wings because this might damage them.

2 With the paper still folded, cut out the shape. Open it up, lay it on thin cardboard, and trace around it.

3 Cut out the cardboard shape and paint the body brown and the wings a bright color. Let dry.

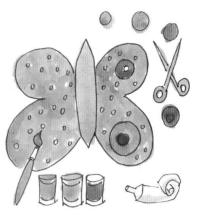

4 Decorate the wings by gluing on circles of colored paper, or paint on lots of colored dots.

5 Turn the butterfly over and tape a small coin to each of the two bigger wings at their widest point.

6 You can balance the butterfly on a pencil or the corner of a table. If it does not work, try moving the coins slightly.

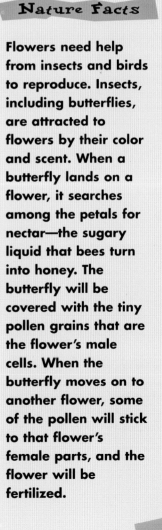

Nature Facts

Flowers need help from insects and birds to reproduce. Insects, including butterflies, are attracted to flowers by their color and scent. When a butterfly lands on a flower, it searches among the petals for nectar—the sugary liquid that bees turn into honey. The butterfly will be covered with the tiny pollen grains that are the flower's male cells. When the butterfly moves on to another flower, some of the pollen will stick to that flower's female parts, and the flower will be fertilized.

Bottle bird feeder

1 Ask an adult to make holes in an empty plastic bottle. Make two holes opposite each other near the top of the bottle and two opposite each other near the bottom. Now make more holes in the sides. Check that they are large enough for a twig to go through.

Birds will get used to feeding in your garden, so keep the container filled up with nuts.

Feather picture

2 Take a stick and push it through the two holes near the top of the bottle. Cut a second one with a forked end and push this through the two holes near the bottom.

1 Collect feathers when you are out walking. Tail feathers tend to have flat ends and wings are more pointed. Draw some birds and color them in.

2 Trim the feathers down if they are too big for the birds you have drawn, then glue them to the picture.

3 Take the lid off the bottle and fill it with nuts or seeds. Put the lid back on.

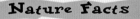

4 Tie a piece of string around the top of the bottle and hang it from the branch of a tree, outside a window or on a balcony. The birds will be able to stand on the twigs and peck through the holes at the nuts.

Nature Facts

If you look at birds sitting on a rooftop, you will notice that they space themselves out evenly along its edge. Birds know to perch exactly one wingspan's distance from the other birds perched beside them so that their wings will not clash when they fly away together.

131

Coconut bird feeder

1 Ask an adult to make a hole in the top of a coconut and two holes on each side around the middle. Drain out the milk. When the coconut has been cut in half, take out the coconut flesh.

2 Thread a long piece of thick string through the hole at the top. Tie lots of big knots in the end of the string so that it will not slip out. The coconut shell should hang like an upside down bell.

3 Ask an adult to pour some leftover cooking fat into the coconut shell. Let it cool and harden.

Hang a bird feeder in your garden and watch the acrobatics of the birds that come to eat from it. Birds can die of starvation during the winter because there aren't many insects around for them to eat, and seeds and berries are scarce. Birds will appreciate the extra food.

4 Tie two pieces of string though the side holes and fasten a thick twig between them to make a swing for the birds to rest on.

5 Hang the feeder from the branch of a tree, outside a window or on a balcony where pets cannot reach it. You might need the help of an adult to do this.

Nature Facts

In the spring, frogs, toads and newts travel to nearby ponds to breed. For a few months, a single pond may contain the eggs, larvae and offspring of these amphibians. Some large ponds contain fish, as well as freshwater mussels, limpets and water snails. Several kinds of worms can live in large numbers, even in the most polluted waters. There may also be some crustaceans, like crayfish or freshwater shrimp living in ponds. Many insects live in fresh water and spend their lives underwater. Some flying insects just lay their eggs there. To spot the microscopic animals that live in ponds, you will need a magnifying glass.

Pond

1 To make a simple garden pond, dig a hole about 1 ft (30 cm) deep. Ask permission first.

2 Line it with very thick plastic sheeting. Make sure that you leave about 10 in (25 cm) around the edge.

3 Pile some big rocks around the edge of the pond to hold down the plastic sheeting.

You will need the help of an adult with this project.

4 Fill the pond with fresh water.

5 Cover any plastic that is showing with soil. Plant small plants and seeds between the rocks. Add fish to the pond. Don't forget to feed them and bring them inside for the winter.

133

Hawk birdscarer

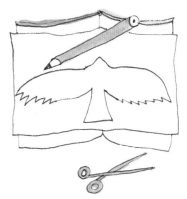

1 Trace the outline of the hawk from this book onto thin paper and cut it out.

4 Ask an adult to straighten out a wire hanger, leaving the hook in place. If you do not have a hanger, use a piece of strong wire.

2 Lay the paper pattern on a piece of very thick cardboard. Trace around it, then cut it out.

3 Paint the shape black or a very dark color. Let dry. Turn it over and paint the other side.

5 Push the wire through the middle of the hawk and bend up the end with pliers—you might need help to do this.

6 Tape the end of the wire to the hawk, then paint over the tape.

7 Hang the hawk where it will scare birds away from vegetable gardens, fruit bushes and delicate plants. It will also keep noisy birds away from your room if you hang it outside your window.

Credits

With thanks to John Stevenson, Mrs Jeannine Songhurst, Henry Stevenson, Bridget and David Atkins, and Daphne Stevenson.